The Quest

By

George A. Hart

ISBN: 978-0-9840313-6-8

Notes

I wrote this book when I was around 18 to 19, maybe 20. It's is one of my first books still written in my first poetic and song style. I have changed very little of this book, mainly some corrections.

Chapter 1

Prism

V-1

During the beginning life was a test.
A test of survival.
Evolving we separated forming different groups.
Now not much as survival.
For life is just being the best at everything.
There is no reality.
We have seen the truth of life being it as we see.
They're living in a dream reality.

V-2

We have evolved beyond the evolving
We have come to the end of evolvement within the flesh.
We have taken the next step beyond.
We have broken the dream reality that our ancestors formed to survive.
Being we are men of metal.

V-3

We are the survivors.
We are the chosen.
We are superior beings of a new life form.
We are the believers.
We are the new world as you see.
During the end of which there is no end.
We are the existence of an eternity.

Earth

V-1

We are the creed of blood an fire.
We are good we are evil.
We are life we are death.
We are mortal we are immortal.
We are justice we are injustice.
We are complete.

V-2

We live in the world denied.
To live is to die.
By seeking truth you defy the law.
For there's no truth to existence.
You are here for now an forever.
Eternal alternate rift through hell.

V-3

Take the right path to your individual source.
Believe thoughts in your mind.
Control your self conscious.
Your life meaningless as seems.
Is destined to greatness.
Join the legion that speaks truth, honor, loyalty.
In time we've grown to withstand attack.
For now we show all the power we know.
Being we are the kings to earth.
Drental Asile the overlord.

Wind

V-1

Wind of life soaring above.
Stand with it not against.
Flow an rise.
Let your mind loose to fly.
Float to the heavens.
The calm breeze to live by.

V-2

Don't fight it or feel its might.
Hear the hurricane of delight.
Feel the power.
Stand with it an unite.
The Quest, we'll never fail.

V-3

Made of gases seen not by the naked eyes.
With out it we would not exist.
Fortune we see gold in what we breathe.
Precious to all for it is free.

V-4

From the four corners of earth.
The endless flow formed above the sky.
North, south, east, west.
The four winds blow.
A compass directed to hell.

V-5

Follow an journey.
To the ends of the earth.
Find your soul.
For it's metal it will glow.

V-6

Life to death.
The wind will know.
Harmony an peace to go.
By time the wind will cover your skull.
Buried alive the undead.
Death to life again.
Feel the breeze of life.
Feel the breeze of death.
Feel eternity indismissed.

Fire

V-1

Beyond the earth the sun illuminates our day.
An the stars mark our path at night.
Under the earth boils up new life.
The hell fire burns.

V-2

The Dragon once thought as a myth.
In ancient times it appeared out of the dark.
Swooping down on villages.
Spitting fire from its mouth.
Destroying everything in its path.
It came from the feared minds of men.
Feeding on their fear.
Then the brave warrior came an defeated it.
Bearing a sword and shield.
Man feared it no more.
So it disappeared from the face of the earth.

V-3

The eternal fire must be kept lit.
For the deadly Dragon might reappear.
Burning day an night keeping all safe.
From the evil that lurks in the darkness.
Guarded by virgins to keep it burning.
See through the fire see the vision of temptation.

V-4

For temptation is good.
Man was tempted to be brave.
He slayed the Dragon an survived.
Survived just one more test.
The tests of fire.

V-5

Down from the sky.
Crashing upon the Earth.
Man still fears this powerful might.
For it is lightning then thunder.
Pure energy sent from the gods.

Chapter 2

Water

V-1

It covers three fourths of the earth.
All life on the planet evolved from it.
An with out it we could not exist.
For we are made of still calm water which we drink.
It's like wine a river of wine.
Endless as it seems it may soon dry up to nothingness.
The wisdom of the ancients tells us to seek beyond.
For these are the tests of water.

V-2

We sailed the seas an crossed the oceans.
We gone beneath them an explored them.
But did we learn their secrets?
To life-to death.

V-3

Beyond an beyond.
Searching through lifespans.
Here again we find the void of eternal secrets.
Now we show the world.
Gravity is side ways into do you see.
Eternal movement on a platform of hallucinations.
As we are an experiment.
Frozen in a mighty circle enclosed.

Blood

V-1

Blood the supplement of water.
Redefined beings of flesh.
Interfaced to survive.
The blood of earth.
In men, animals, creatures.
The essence of life.

V-2

Sworn by it.
Death by it.
Live by it.
The blood flows eternally.

V-3

Consisted of destiny.
Your lives are destined to survive.
Even at the ends of time.
When the earth is destroyed.
The sun falls to darkness.
Our universe collapses into the black hole of infinity.
We will survive to live on.
To rebuild new life.

Flesh

V-1

The derangement of self fulfillment.
Figurating death to your advantage.
We see beyond the virtue of life itself.
Contact the soul upon the grave.
Picturing the defilement of your own death.
See yourself without flesh.

V-2

Immortality is what we show you.
Transformed inner existence.
Directed to all life forms.
You are alive you are dead the same.
Through an around the source of time.

V-3

Metal is the key.
To new survival.
Eternity we'll live.
Without flesh no bounds to hold us back.
Free to triumph over our ancestors.

Metal

V-1

The inscriptions of gods.
We took the flesh away.
Reborn metal again.
Into do you see?
The beacon of steel.
For we are living metal.

V-2

To the end we take the knowledge.
Known to man all that is here an now.
By the world we're born
By the world we breed.
By the world we come.
Then by the world we'll go.

V-3

Go to the light.
By metal.
No more need for flesh.
Pain, death, sorrow.
Infinity lies ahead.

Men

V-1

We are men.
We are flesh.
We are blood.
We are of metal.

V-2

Men live, men die.
Men scream, an men lie.
We as men take the oath.
With blood we swear by our lives.
Even if it's suicide.

V-3

To the earth we're bound.
To hell we're stranded.
Now by our cause we trust an trust no more.
Evolution we open a new door.
Soon we alone shall explore.

V-4

Men of earth.
We call to you now.
Join the quest of life an survival.
Come to our hand.
Abide by our laws of humanity.
Seek glory, righteousness, majesty.
Become one with or without the body.
Create eternity amongst our selves.
Unite an become one with all.

V-5

Dust to dust.
Ashes to ashes.
The dirt is where you risen from.
An the dirt is where you'll return.
If you continue your own existence.
In the grounds of life as you know.
For you we open the path of eternal life.

Chapter 3

Evil

V-1

Evil is what you believe it to be.
It can be right to one an wrong to another.
We believe they equally balanced.
They should be combine to be one.
As all separations should.

V-2

The evil that men do.
Unlike good it's patronized for its beliefs
We live evil in our lives.
We live good in our lives.
We love to equalize.
Without good evil would not exist.
Without evil good would not exist.
Without balance we will decay an desist.

V-3

Turn away the beliefs you hold.
Behold wisdom, strength, power.
See the new way.
Join the realm an take away the insanity.

Good

V-1

Good evil they are but the same.
Teach the children our way.
Fear not the world's false facts.
Their beliefs of how the world should turn.
Then fear not the true facts.
Our beliefs of how the world will turn.

V-2

In the light in the darkness.
Hold forth your knowledge.
To this hidden belief.
You are free saved souls of imprisonment.
Wander to them lose the being with in your self.
False gods they call to you.
Now call no more.
For we are already worshipping a new lord.
Some say it's a true god.
Some say it's the worship of your selves.
Some say it's a symbol of new life.
But we say it's all but as one united society.
Living free to your will, soul, flesh, blood, metal.
Free to survive united.

Light

V-1

How we see in the day.
An what brightens our path at night.
May it be man made or the sun.
It's what we all call light.

V-2

But there is another light beyond.
A light known not to most men.
The source of power.
In the light of the world of our god.
An altered dimension set aside.
For all who see the light.

V-3

Again it's one part of a balanced unit.
Drawn from the depths within.
Day then night, night then day.
Light to dark, dark to light.
For it is a dark light in the light dark.

Darkness

V-1

Darkness, it fills the space.
The space known as light.
In the shadows lurks the evil of good.
An in the light lurks the good of evil.
Demons of light an darkness.
We are the minds of the earth.
We are what is unknown to ourselves.
We know the end of self sacrifice.
As to help others understand.
Which they don't understand themselves.
We will an are showing you what we know.
Of the earth an all there is to know about life.
As we learn more an more ourselves.
As we step beyond our own boundaries.

V-2

Through darkness we see light.
Through light we see darkness.
Through both we see the power of eternal existence.
Existing beyond the edge.
Counter acting each source.
Balancing the scales of life.

V-3

Sent through the mystic fog.
The void of gray nothingness.
Shattering sparks of light an dark.
Mapping the afterlife through the black light.

V-4

Turning side by side.
Wrenching the fearless in our grip.
Now we let you see an let you choose.
Your own life an eternity.

V-5

Through the wasteland.
Undivided we march the endless plain.
Searching where no man dares.
Defying the unwritten law.
We stand beyond the edge of space an time.
Dimensions to worlds to underworlds.
Set aside for those who seek the un-seeking.
But sought the found seeker of life.

Fear

V-1

Fear of life fear of death.
Fear in men's hearts.
You fear to nothing you know unexplained.
Except for the un-expecting.
You know not what you fear but fear itself.
An the pain that comes with it.
For that itself perceives all who see not what we see.

V-2

Feeling pain may it be physical or mental.
To know pain is to know life.
With fear an pain behind us.
All knowing endless depths.
We now conquer fear with our mind.
An with our heart the pain will soon end.

V-3

We shall never fear no more.
Never to fear life.
Never to fear death.
An never to fear the unknown to be known.
The afterlife or to fear mortality itself.
For immortality we shall teach all.

Chapter 4

Life

V-1

We live together.
We live alone.
To be alive to roam free.
To cleanse the soul with life again.

V-2

Without flesh we saw beyond the light.
Dread dark forces live evil with eternal life.
By metal an by the sword of black light.
Around the earth rides the knight of steel.
With shining armour an a mighty shield.
Battling lifeless angels before time begun.
From the other side under the black sun we fly.
Once again now we'll die alive.
In the wasteland of all are lives.

V-3

By the land by the sky by the world we live.
Then by it we die to the earth we cry.
Tear not the soul in the vows of death.
For to live eternity breaks no law of life.

V-4

Henceforth the world of gold.
Widespread new wars to live on.
Arrow of light in our sight.
Death to life by metal we unite.
Contributing brothers to our cause.
From the dust an ashes we rise.
Peace an harmony for all who side.
With our new law of life.
Being this is the quest to trust an recite.

V-5

Through Self fulfillment an sinister acts.
One way or another the fight will never end.
Forced to surrender in the light.
A dream that will come in the night.
One working unit to control an operate.
For they are an will be the people of metal.
An that is what you are.
If you believe in these mighty words.

Death

V-1

We live death to walk to the light.
In the dark death of living light.
The guards watch the gate of dark light.
Die in one world to live another life.
Not reincarnated to live to die then live again.
Not reincarnation but re-death of re-life.
To believe the unbelieving is to see the light.
Light of day to breathe the air of earth.
An live to die un-inert.

V-2

Beyond the darkness of new death.
Lies the new hope of life eternally.
Hidden to those who live in the reality.
Reality of their own lives bound to earth.
In the flesh they see not the source.
From the depths of believe in eternal peace.
In death as to life itself we know not eternity.
For eternity is our strength an ultimate goal.
Now we step into the once barren void.

Believers

V-1

Believe onto the end.
For if you believe there shall be no end.
You shall live eternal existence.
Death is no cause to die.
That's one step beyond the gate.
Where here you're bound to life.
An there you're bound to the life of the dead.
Seek beyond this live the life of the undead.
An behold you are the believers.

V-2

Sold on fear but fear not the end.
Believe in a mighty fate.
If you believe to die then die.
For this is life or death in your world.
In this world we believe in eternal life.
But we shall never fear the end.
We believe not the end of end.
But the beginning to not the end.

Unbelievers

V-1

Through all life the unbeliever exists.
He who is non-believing is forbidden.
Forbidden to the secrets we know.
For the unbeliever will not believe.
Facts to us an fiction to them.
If you are this you are the believing unbelieving.

V-2

You are helpless against your own death.
You fear what lies beyond.
An you have no hope for the future.
You do believe you are normal.
The reality you live is gone.
We broke the dream reality.
An your world exploded from within.
You do not an did not believe.
We left you in the cold.
While we moved on to eternity.
Now you suffer the end which we shall never have.
For the quest is what you seek an what we sought.

Heaven

V-1

Heaven a kingdom beyond the sky.
To the bounds of eternity we see not the gates.
But a wall no entrance no exit.
Only the soul can see or pierce this mighty wall.
Through this we see another kingdom not far.
But they are one a kingdom within a kingdom.

V-2

We hear a voice the voice of our god.
For two thousand years it's never been told.
An now we have the strength to tell all.
Hear the words of a true god.
For he was flesh long ago in his mortality.
Now in his immortality he reigns from a new kingdom.
A kingdom within it flows from holy to unholy.
Accepting all who believe for eternity.

V-3

Hear me my people seek another kingdom.
For that which I leave is too small for me.
Join together as one live life eternity.
An even in the death of life I'll be there.
To guide you through to my kingdom.
For my kingdom is yours an mine as one.

Hell

V-1

Hell the underworld of sinners.
Who did not repent to the god of life an death.
What shall they do join a new legion.
Where fire an ice are no bounds for a prison.
An believe in eternal hear an there.
Free of torment onto your soul.
For life is the worship of death.
Being death is life an life is death.
From world to world.

V-2

This is the kingdom within a kingdom.
It is one, one to another many kingdoms.
Beyond the wall you will see.
To eternity within the realm.
The sight of a kingdom with no boundaries.
An no laws accept belief.
For this is the legend of the kingdom within.
An the god of eternity.

Chapter 5

Space

V-1

Between space to space opposite the void.
But much like it as its depths are endless.
Four dimensions to the continuum.
Where we find the earth rotating on its axis.
Length, width, height, and time.
The space an time continuum.

V-2

The space around our lives moves freely.
Through each meeting to another being.
As we intertwine to the physical laws.
Searching for the link between us.
In the spiritual being to death as life.
The key lies hear within the pages of the quest.

V-3

Space an time strand by strand.
The fibers of individual knowledge.
We see the terror of forced peace.
That leads to war an destruction.
Then again the tremble of time awakens.
For change is inevitable to survival.
We take one more step to immortality.
An the fulfillment of the quest.

Time

V-1

Continuing, altering, ever changing.
Our world turns ever more under the yellow sun.
As do we as we mold the earth to its undying end.
Crescent moon of lust for life free to harness power.
The greed of wealth an power exceeds time.
Never ending the unit of time.

V-2

Soaring time of the inner soul.
The truth says we dare cross time.
Through it the world unfolds.
We see ourselves through this mirror.
The image tells all that times been here before.
When the door is open another key you'll find.
This is time all around us.
The dimension that goes forward an back.
That sends us in an out of the world we chose.
To the worlds that exist simultaneous with ours.
Find your line an live eternity in time.

War

V-1

We see their end a holocaust of blinding light.
In the aftermath we see the cold darkness.
Descending upon the lifeless stricken world.
As we still survive to rise from beneath.
We grasp the world in our sights.
To rebuild the new life eternal.

V-2

War the opposite of peace.
Fighting for life the sacrifice of men.
Through death an sorrow an defeat.
The surrender of your sacred land.
Death before dishonor or peace before slaughter.

V-3

Lost souls on the front of doom.
In the dark sight of human despair.
Lies new hope beyond the barrier.
Crumbling justice back at command.
The orders of power leave new evidence.
Maintaining control the leaders ignore all.
As the ordinance of the people decide their own fate.
A new legion is awaiting.

Immortality

V-1

Man dies in his world he was born.
Lived full an un-full he seems immortal.
Through his children he lives on.
An to leave behind all that waste.
Man was meant to rule it's in the genes.
But to rule together as one.
Though he knows he'll die if there was another way.
Would he choose this way or would it be better to die.
That's what we showing you here in the quest.
For this is the spiritual guide.
An this is the question an answer of immortality.
The choice lies in your hands together.

V-2

Immortality to live the eternity of time.
To learn the secrets of life an death.
To see beyond all other false explanations to life.
Showing those that what they seek is within one whole.
The human mind the source of self knowledge.
The world has never seen or felt this sense.
It's time to complete the quest.

Chapter 6

Justice

Without justice there's no unity.
An without unity there's no justice.
The world lives un-unified an unjustified.
Through this they lost control under the vows of eternal life.
They live in certain chaos.
Never to understand true knowledge of life an death.
An see beyond the reality they live.

V-2

Justice is unity in this we live on.
To overcome any obstacles in life.
To see evermore into the light beyond.
While others see nothing in what we see.
Their lost eternally in the ultimate in their self built chaos.
When they run from it all it follows them to haunt them.
To plague them through time from life to life to death.
Unless they choose to follow in the footsteps of eternity.

V-3

Once man sees this fact to understand is to see new life.
The life that man never lived an soon will.
While the world tumbles we shall move ahead.
An leave them in their own underworld of the wasteland.
The world they created on their own separated an alone.

Rights

V-1

Rights of men living or dead are seen.
Seeing as to the fulfillment of life as to death.
The last rights of man are acknowledged in order.
Through their own judgment of life as we know it.

V-2

We see that man's rights are blurred in vein.
Under written laws of earth.
By tortured men of lost hearts.
An enduring certain obligated fates.
Through the bloody barren mischief caught within us.
The gates of tangible force.
Allow existing mentors the rights of destruction.
To those not seen in the light.

V-3

Once caught among separate unities.
They lost in time the true meaning of equal division.
Now to be reunited they must learn knowledge.
The knowledge of the ancients.
For that which they learn is crumbling.
Learn both together as one an again you'll see beyond.
All knowing this the rights of man are equal.

Judgment

V-1

Walk on through eons of life.
Abroad the soldiers of fate are awaiting.
In the dark dream of reality.
The saint of doom arises in the robe of fire.
No mortal man can pierce this being.
He sees an judges all not for actions but for beliefs.
The rings of fire the holy masquerade to damnations beyond.
The catalysts of terror corrode evermore into the light.
One to one the ice lands meet parading new emblems to honor.
For this is Judgment an you are the judge.

V-2

Bound to eternity live no lie or die the eternal death.
From hell from here from within jagged sabers glittering agony.
To long lasting peace true of harsh senseless wars.
We shall no not destruction to ourselves.
An may the power flow equally.
Therefore religion speaks an the Mask will have mercy on you.

Destruction

V-1

Lethal weapon of bodily harm.
Pounding your mind with thoughts never thought before.
Blood an guts the terror of eternal epoch.
The battle of total an complete death.
The end of eternity as we know it.
For this is absolute destruction.

V-2

Dooms day lives on an the future is here.
The detonation of the world soon we'll see for ourselves.
What are fate is or shall be.
Nuclear war can happen anytime no one will know.
While preparing new preparations of the world.
We collect the knowledge that is needed for survival.
An create it to survive eternity.

V-3

If you don't disintegrate in the explosion.
The shock wave will tear through the body without notice.
Your bones will be crushed into pieces.
An your organs will explode instantly.
Every ounce of blood an liquid in your body will have dried up.
Now you are a slivery mass of dead cells.
An this is your actual course of destruction.

Power

V-1

The power is gained in many ways.
It depends on what you call power.
There's physical power or mental power.
An the capacity or moral ability an to think.
We now see new strength in life an during death.
The death of the flesh as we live on in metal.
Metal is man metal is machine metal is power an metal is eternity.
An this is the cyber man complete.

V-2

Feel new essence of life hidden in the pages of the quest.
There are verses of power rituals an incantations.
To help those in need of strength an energy to overcome.
An become refreshed of new self knowledge an awareness.
To see beyond the light an through the void.
An to have ever lasting trust in the quest.
For it shall never fail you.

V-3

This is power to know to share.
We show all the basis of true power.
An the knowledge to complete it.
While surviving an eternity.

Religion

V-1

Many beliefs have evolved around the world.
Forming false images to hate an disregard.
Though there are many different people.
There is one god with many names an beliefs.
An to believe in one is to have religion.

V-2

From the beginning man worshiped gods.
An now in the space age more than ever.
Being now there's a god all can believe in.
But he was always there an his name has changed.
An the beliefs have changed to one combined.

V-3

To survive the years to come unity is near.
The fate of man is beyond death.
Beyond the fire from the sky.
Through eternity life is reborn.
An our kingdom is yours an yours ours.
For they are one it also has many names.
In the realm side by side we stand united.
The world is one by land by sea by air.

Mask

V-1

Howling violence over testimony.
Sleeping never resisting.
Temple of arms seeping justice.
Through the cracks of damnations.
We lust the ancient gauges of power.
Howling terror out of the Mask.

V-2

Anarchy imposing on the law.
We're trapped under their splinters.
Rising strength giving birth.
The mightiest armies walking the earth.

V-3

Simble sod ancient gods.
We call forth to you.
Man is wicked man is cruel.
We see the world wasted to false gods.
For we believe in you.
Rinson Ralon devil may you harm.
Evil riddle wrenched to life wrenched to death.
May you all be possessed.

V-4

Arakia lies beyond.
Here us now or never live on.
Anjase ankan best ries.
We've changed our minds.
Take your souls an begone.
Masile entisle weaken.
We don't give in.
Demon spies an evil lies.
We like to be immortally revived.
Latis entaves maracus an mighty arramund.
Come to our hand body is sold an so is the mind.
An the souls been stolen.
The flesh we toss to the sea.
Mad arakia mad as can be.
A limits been set.
We can no longer be free.
The new justice maker is the one called the Mask.

V-5

There are many pieces to the puzzling quest.
An many songs poems to be heard an learned.
For this is the song of the Mask.

V-6

Hungry violence seeker.
Coming through the trees.
Soaring as he pleases.
Latch your doors board your windows.
Hungry violence seeker.
Hiding his face where ever he goes.
Leaving nothing to be seen.
Slashing through your house.
Tearing the flesh from within.
Hungry violence seeker.
Flies through the wind.
He searches your next of kin.

Chapter 7

Satan

V-1

The bleeding terror from within.
No man can tolerate the fear an pain.
By the incantation of darkness await the soul.
Completion made to die await not the soldier.
Ride evermore in the dark light of Eve.
Send not your precious life but send the world.
An drop to your knees upon the gates of hell.
To strike vengeance the last resort.
Beyond infinity below an above an upon the earth.
The lord in another name that many know.
For he is the almighty god called Satan.

V-2

Demon of fire rise through me.
Bring us strength bring us energy.
Dameian of the dark moon return us with power.
An souls of damnations are resting eternally.
Above the abyss an beyond we see the eternal destiny.
Mark this one with never ending immortality.
All who join by our side shall see true to the dragon.
The eyes who call for us in darkness of light.
He who is him of all powerful an might.
Through this we see new light beyond.
Dark lord we will hold all light of day or night.
As we will fight for eternity.

God

V-1

He is one he is all he is true he is complete.
For one to rule proof he's shown us.
Through eternity justice commands he.
Running blood burning afire.
The world is a whole society.
Living properly the way we see eternity.
The tests have shown true power.
One by one they've judged to seek one.
The keepers of the earth to watch over infinity.
An now the time has come to complete the eternal quest.

V-2

To our god we leave the world to crush if we fail.
For we shall never fail we trust the quest within us.
Freedom is at hand to last we shall prevail.
To us we leave eternity as our souls float back to earth.
As death is no end we shall reunite again.
In life we see death to escape to run free.
New survival an immortality seeking truth you see.
The knowledge completing eternity.
By your own destiny the temptation exists.

Knowledge

V-1

The world we see afire in superimposed chaos.
Fighting back death an new life to come.
Send the youth reborn again to rebuild all.
Toward injustice the world cries one tear.
To show willing character to trust ones image.
Through this creation we see their end lost without the quest.

V-2

One alone await the scream to complete in war.
Their world the same over infinity change is necessary.
To complete one with eternity.
The end is near their end which we'll never fear.
Why do we care are world is here.
Now we rise from the dust freedom of corruption.
An blood to reveal our new society hidden beneath.

V-3

Knowledge to us like money is worshipped.
Thrown to hell the earth is now one within all.
Yours an ours the knowledge combined.
Be the one with one to know yourself forever bonded.
To one to us to yourself to all as one.
By the final test to complete the quest.

Survival

V-1

Taste of flesh taste of death taste to us.
Our survival is indefinite to reign among ourselves.
An inevitably to happen for we are the human being.
Fighting wars to solve problems an creating them.
Senseless meaning less harming endangering all.
An the planet itself is hopelessly doomed by man.
One more time millennium returned to depths below.
To primitive life once again.
The earth has many ways of dealing with our formation.
It can alter all our lives bring them to a halt.
Never seeing it until it's too late an the end is all that's left.
Eternity means survival without survival there's no eternity.
An the quest has fallen an burnt in our own ashes.
For destiny is in our grasp take hold an never let go.
As to we must survive eternity.

Destiny

V-1

A great fire burns deep inside all.
Dreams of the future to come forth.
The wait through your life feels endless.
An you know something big is awaiting you.
For this is your destiny now take control.

V-2

Follow eternity in metal call to justice.
Reanimate your existence from flesh.
Remember these beliefs an teach them to the new ones to come.
An never again will it be the same.
Grant refuge among our walls.
Forever forget the old religions or combine them with one.

V-3

See destiny an see it well.
Look beyond toward from hell.
A coward set upon this tail.
No joke build his hope an see your own eternity.
This is the lost reality where the cowardly one ran.
To the crack of doom in it he saw into the eternal fire.
He feared no more as he saw all as the face of our lord.
For this is the tail of destiny that each one seeks.
An that which we sought an see our destiny.
Being that which you'll never imagine.
That to when your quest is fulfilled.

Chapter 8

Temptation

V-1

Brain less tormenter.
Never missing, ever resisting, severing eternity.
His judgment to the key.
Forth fitting your misery.
Carving sanely into your sanity.
Never hearing, ever seeing, severing your unity.
Choosing the calm barrier within.
You lose the normal selfless one.
Standing alone facing life in the cold wind.
Taking your mind deep within your soul beyond.
Now lost you wake to this terrorizing dream.
Test your fate to resist the horror of your own death.
Last chance to escape this theft.
Take the next step rip open your reality.
Look it inside out an see where you went wrong.
Trust the one you know alone now see your misery blown away.
Caught among flesh recreate, rebuild, reunite, your reality.
New an complete the life you made on your own.
Follow yourself controlled thoughts you wish to come true.
An see the quest become one with you.

Eternity

V-1

Never bound to earthly torture.
Together as one an trusted by blood.
Never shall we separate are bondage.
Warm the breath kept in one.
Greater the mass greater the strength.
An feel blissed to us of your eternity.
Alone your dealt the cards of life.
An alone you closed your deal.
What's left of your life nothing but death you thought.
Then you've seen the light an now quest has been chosen.
For you who have the heart an sight to see an feel pain.

V-2

Feel it no more but feel that which is your own eternity.
Seen through many prophets eyes their salvation.
To whom world trembles for alone they call an become evil.
Escaping fleeing their own treachery that which they don't see.
Luxury is shown to have its own taste within.
For it is you from what you are made an what you've earned.
Learning new life an patience to grant.
For we give you endless eternity to live free.
Enjoying your eternal immortality.

Love

V-1

Together an sided as one seeking unity.
An that which you found now seek beyond truth.
See beyond death to kill for to murder eliminate.
For that which you did for is powerful the deception of love.

V-2

For love is the worship of each one to that you see fire.
Feel fire created fire in depths below us fires burn.
An upon the earth but this is a burning fire within.
Desire of one to share your own life with bonded as one.

V-3

Though this can rupture an explode within a heart beat.
Take serious actions think it through an conclude it.
See the mistake an thrash it from your life.
Remember your youth see instant heart brokenness.
It can sting an stun an amputate or ravage eternally.
Test your love test it within see it clear see it well.
There you'll see your fate bound to eternity.
Burst it open with your reality strip it clean.
Stitch it one by one closed an sealed never revealed.
Love is healed an unhealed.

Pain

Pain among all of us for this is life.
An pain is just one part to live your life.
Without it we see no world an no life.
But the pain within must be put aside.
By this you'll feel free again an once more feel new life.
Now see with us the world as one an the pain now removed.
An your living without fear of what's beyond.
See justice true of false errors an mistakes to destroy life.
For this is the new reality we bring an share to all.
Being pain is within all who see eternity.
An now we the wise teach you to see without flesh.
Your movement through space an air filling you with energy.
To make conclusions within to judge your own life.
For the pain is coarse knowledge proving your existence.
You live here upon earth this speaks to all.
No man can prove this wrong being your living in eternity.
Through space an time vortexes eternity is ours an yours.
One we live in pain to run is to die alone.
Stay unite with blood an bond to the quest.
Now see your eternity come with us an feel pain no more.

Wasteland

V-1

An in their end the world they created alone.
Their destructions been seen through us an others.
They lost their selves an bound to fall eternally.
In their world they built alone we watch an wait.
It crumbles around them without notice.
They see not their own end which has been shown to them.
As they disappear from the earth they leave their plague.
In their world as ours for they have created the wasteland.

V-2

By darkness enfades to evil the earth is given to us as one.
Our worlds have created power an the ultimate societies.
An now the earth is one with the quest an itself.
Forever united never to fall we live without death.
To harness the eternal life amongst one being to whom is you.
That is all that see the light beyond.
Which brightens every day of our lives.
For every day that we believe an it shall never dim or fade.
So we must not let world be hindered into the forbidden wasteland again.
That which we live in the reality that they don't see.
Given knowledge of eternity take care an do by it well.
An never shall it betray you or never you betray it.
Seeing evermore into the light never forgetting the quest.
For it shall never end therefore you shall never know the end.

www.ingramcontent.com/pod-product-compliance
Lightning Source LLC
Chambersburg PA
CBHW081157090426
42736CB00017B/3371